THE FIRST GENERATION MINDSET

Unlocking Success in Your Life and Business with 3 Simple Steps

By Kunal Seth

© 2023 2MARKET MEDIA

ISBN: 979-8-218-24685-3

Published by 2MARKET MEDIA with Kunal Seth

For everyone who has taken a leap of faith

Contents

INTRODUCTION 1

PART 1: VISION 7

CHAPTER 1: WHAT IS THE FIRST GENERATION MINDSET? 9

CHAPTER 2: HOW TO USE THE FIRST-GENERATION
MINDSET FOR THE FUTURE 25

CHAPTER 3: PUTTING VISION INTO PRACTICE 39

PART 2: VALUE 57

CHAPTER 4: UNDERSTANDING VALUE 59

CHAPTER 5: HOW TO SELL YOUR VALUE AND
CAPITALIZE ON IT 71

PART 3: ASK 79

CHAPTER 6: THE HISTORY OF THE ASK—HOW
PEOPLE APPROACH THE ASK 81

CHAPTER 7: BELIEVING IN YOUR "ASK" 93

CHAPTER 8: CRAFTING AND APPLYING "THE ASK" 99

CHAPTER 9: HONEST MEASUREMENT
           AND ACCOUNTABILITY 105

CHAPTER 10: UPDATING YOUR VISION
            AND CRAFTING YOUR LEGACY 111

BONUS CHAPTER: CULTURAL TRAINING 117

Introduction

Welcome to the transformative world of the "First Generation Mindset." In these pages, we will embark on a transformative journey that transcends borders, cultures, and circumstances. As a successful real estate entrepreneur who immigrated from India to the United States, I stand as a living testament to the power of a resolute mindset—one that thrives on Vision, Value, and the Ask.

Deep within the hearts of first-generation immigrants lies a fierce determination to make their mark on a new land. It is a mindset born of unyielding resolve, propelled by the desire to shape a brighter future. *This mindset is not limited to the first-generation alone,* for it is a philosophy that can inspire and motivate individuals from all walks of life. It is the embodiment of the belief that dreams are achievable with the right vision, dedication, and the courage to ask for what one deserves. As you will see from my own story, it took me many years to create the framework that had helped me persevere through hard times.

In this book, we will explore the three core components of the First Generation Mindset: Vision, Value, and Ask. Each component, like the intricate pieces of a puzzle, contributes to the larger picture of success. It is through understanding and applying these elements that you can create a life of purpose, prosperity, and lasting impact. I have broken the book into three distinct sections to help you master each one.

A vision is the compass that guides us toward our goals, fueling our actions and inspiring perseverance in the face of adversity. But how do we cultivate a clear vision that propels us toward greatness? The answer lies in visualizing our dreams, seeing them as tangible possibilities, and manifesting them into reality.

You are bound to encounter mental roadblocks in the form of limiting beliefs. These beliefs can cripple your potential and hinder progress. I will share personal anecdotes of my mental roadblocks and how I broke free from their shackles. Vision alone is not enough; it must be met with unwavering effort and dedication. The first-generation mindset thrives in a relentless pursuit of excellence. By investing our time and energy in the pursuit of our vision, we lay the foundation for our success.

Value is the cornerstone of success in any endeavor. By thinking from an outsider's perspective, we can better grasp what others truly value, thereby creating bridges between our aspirations and theirs. This profound understanding of value empowers us to become invaluable forces in our chosen fields.

Creating value for others is the secret to success. We will delve into elevating our value-add and bridging the gaps that separate us from our goals. By elevating ourselves and how we can provide what someone else needs, we become catalysts for positive change in our life.

Asking is an intrinsic part of the human experience, but not everyone knows how to ask effectively. We'll explore the art of asking in a manner that aligns with our vision and the value we bring to others. By explaining our aspirations and the value we bring, we can increase the likelihood of receiving a positive response.

Asking effectively is an art form—one that requires finesse, sincerity, and prior value provision. I delve into the process of making the ask when we have already demonstrated our worth. We explore practical scripts and techniques to frame our requests in a way that resonates with our audience. By reiterating our vision and the value we bring, we become architects of our success.

As we accomplish milestones on our journey, we must regularly evaluate our progress, reassess our vision, and redefine success. By understanding that sub-visions contribute to the larger picture, we ensure that our efforts remain relevant and impactful. The first-generation mindset embraces this practice of honest measurement and accountability, propelling us ever forward.

In the final chapter of this empowering journey, we explore the concept of legacy—a lasting impact that extends beyond ourselves. By taking inventory periodically and refreshing our vision, we set the stage for a legacy that echoes through generations. As first-generation individuals, we understand the significance of passing on not just material wealth but the values that define our success.

As a bonus to readers, I have included a chapter detailing my experience in cultural training. You may not be familiar with the same subject, but I believe that you have something that you know about that can bring value to others. I tell this story about evolving into a nationwide trainer to encourage you to explore what makes you unique to others.

As you embark on this path, remember that the power to shape your destiny lies within you. By understanding the essence of Vision, the impact of Value, and the art of the Ask, you will pave the way to a life of purpose and prosperity. So, let us begin this transformative journey together, knowing that the First Generation Mindset has the potential to transcend boundaries and unlock the true greatness within us all.

Kunal Seth

PART 1

VISION

CHAPTER 1

What is the First Generation Mindset?

The only way to get what you want in life is to have the First Generation Mindset. The First Generation Mindset is all about taking nothing for granted and knowing you must create your own future. Wake up every morning motivated and ready to be challenged. It means you have a vision for where you're going, the wherewithal to prove your value, and the guts to ask for what you want. *This mindset applies to you, regardless if you're a first-generation or not, if you're looking for success.* As you go down a generation—second, third, fourth, or fifth generation—people start to take things for granted.

The United States is a young country compared to most. For example, the history of China and Japan traces back over 2,000 years. Austria and France are over 1,000 years old. The United States, on the other hand, isn't even 250 years old. And yet, in that very short span of time, it's become the most economically powerful, innovative country on Earth. How can that be?

Unlike every other nation on the planet, the United States is the only one that's founded not on a singular ethnic or racial identity, not on an ancestral bloodline, but instead on an idea, a concept—and it's a simple one: that all people are created equal and that all people have the right to life, liberty, and the pursuit of happiness. All of this can be yours in this country, with just one condition—you must be ready to work for it.

And for over two hundred years, people from all over the world have accepted this one condition. They've come from Europe, Asia, Africa, Latin, and South America.

They've left everything they've known—their families, their friends, their homes, even their languages—to start a new life, to create something for themselves, something better than what they had before.

This endless influx of immigrants is the lifeblood of America. In fact, each individual immigrant story is also the story of America. There is no America without these brave, ambitious people risking everything for a better life. They brought with them new ideas, new perspectives, and new ways of looking at the world. Whether they came here 200 years ago or 200 days ago, each immigrant to the United States had to have a certain mindset—what I call the First Generation Mindset. It's the mindset of innovation, ingenuity, and progress. The First Generation Mindset is, in effect, fundamental to innovation and success. My three step framework—Vision, Value, Ask—is the roadmap to building and maintaining that success the first-generation way.

I came to this country in 2001 with a whole lot of nothing and have since become an incredibly successful real estate agent, all through my own hard work. Year over year, my real estate company "The Seth Brothers" closes over 300 transactions and 100 million dollars in sales volume every year.

The secret formula that I have applied over all these years is a three-step process—Vision, Value, Ask— that you'll learn in this book. All of us have made "asks" in our lives. We want to ask for a sale, someone to go out on a date with us. We always have an "ask," and we go for the "ask." We are trained, growing up: "Don't give up. Don't take no for an answer." That's a philosophy. My philosophy is about having a vision first, then your value comes next, and then finally comes your "ask," which is what ultimately gets you to your end goal.

CR ƎD

I came to America from India in January 2001 to go to graduate school at Louisiana State University (LSU). I was grateful that my parents were kind enough to give me the money to pay for my tuition for the first year. But before I even came to America, I decided I did not want to depend on my parents. They had done enough for me throughout my life, and I was thankful for all they had given me. But I wanted to make my own mark, to build my career on my own, and I couldn't do that if I was constantly relying on my parents' financial backing. So I decided I would accept their generous offer to pay for the first year, but then I would have to do it all on my own.

Unfortunately, my plan hit an immediate obstacle. For most international students, when coming to America, their first objective is to find a job on campus so that they can start paying for their tuition fees and earn some money for living expenses right away. But my admission letter to LSU indicated that I was admitted on "probation," meaning that I couldn't work on campus.

Upon my arrival at LSU, I boarded with three other students in a temporary accommodation a few weeks before the semester started. Every morning I would wake up, go to campus, and visit all the different academic departments. I would knock on every professor's door in each department in hopes of finding an opportunity to work for them. But door after door, time after time, I kept being told there was nothing available. And every evening, when I would come back home, my roommates would look at me increasingly puzzled. "Kunal, what's wrong with you? On your admission letter, it says that you cannot work on campus. What don't you get about that?"

And I would say, "Let me first find a job. Then I'll worry about what the letter says." And so every day for three weeks straight, I continued to do the same exact thing. I would walk a few miles to campus, go to different departments, and check with any professor who I hadn't seen previously about job openings. And every day I would come back home without a job offer.

Until finally, with only two days left before the semester started, I caught a break. There was an opening in a department for an assistantship. After dozens of rejections, I finally received the opportunity I had been so desperately looking for.

The only problem, of course, was that I wasn't technically allowed to accept an assistantship because of what my acceptance letter said. But as I told my roommates, I had first to get an offer, and then I'd figure out how to get around the prohibition. I decided to send a petition to the Dean of the Business School. He read it over, impressed by my story, hard work, and diligence. He wrote a letter to the Graduate Admission Committee recommending that the clause disallowing me from working on campus be removed and that I be allowed to work in my newly acquired position. The next day, they accepted his recommendation and removed the prohibition, and I finally had my first job in America.

This is a small story, of course. My first big "win" in America didn't find me revolutionizing the tech industry or making millions off a cool new social media app. But immigrant stories are made of millions of stories like this—small stories, humble stories, that advance a person a few feet rather than a few miles. But with each successive story, with each small "win," they advance closer to their goal.

I had achieved what I set out to do, my goal, and my "ask" was responded to with a "yes" because I had proven my value via that petition letter to the Dean. I was given the opportunity to prove my value by having a vision and sticking to it. When you follow the path using vision, value, and "ask" as your guide, a path like a first-generation person follows, amazing things can happen.

Getting a job right away was especially important to me because it was my first step in becoming independent and self-sufficient. If I wanted to live off the support and goodwill of my parents, I could've stayed in India. But that's not what I wanted. I wanted a new life, a different life, and I wanted to create that life all on my own. This is what the First Generation Mindset is all about.

The First Generation Mindset Framework

Having a vision, creating value, and making the "ask"... this is the framework of the First Generation Mindset— ones you too can use to get ahead, first-generation or otherwise.

I hope you can see in my small story of triumph over adversity the energy and motivation I had to find that first job. Rather than relying on my parents for the first year, which I easily could have done, or spending most of my days socializing with my new roommates, which was also tempting, I prioritized securing a job before the difficult academic work of the semester began. I had a vision for myself. I knew I had value. I just had to prove it and make the ask.

But after a full week of rejections and hearing "no, sorry" dozens of times, my energy and motivation waned. In this instance, when things got hard, I needed to rely on my bigger vision of "making it" in this country to keep me going. Keeping your own big vision in mind of the life you want will help you do the same when you hit bumps in the road—that's the First Generation Mindset.

You must visualize being successful. It's the first step, and there's no other way around it. Whatever success means to you, whether it's money in the bank, work-life balance, number of transactions, whatever it may be, you must visualize that. Not only because you need to know what you're working towards but also because you can hold it in your mind when things inevitably become difficult.

As you work towards this vision, you're proving your value. This country loves resilience. We admire and respect people who have a vision and go after it relentlessly. Part of that is seeing what value you can provide to others. If you want something from someone, provide value to them. When you prove your value, you have two legs to stand on to make an "ask" of them. How can someone say no to you when you have given them the value they desire, and you are so clearly capable and hard-working? They can't.

My first "win" in America was not big headline news; rather, it's a humble story of a boy from India securing his first job in a country completely foreign to him. But it was a first step in my big vision of proving my value and making my "asks" that were able to get me to where I am today.

Everyone is First Generation

Like most people do, I've experienced my share of hardship and challenges in life. Not to mention all the smaller daily stressors that can upend your day, which then upend your week, which, before you know it, blows up your month. It's easy to get derailed in this life. Every one of us needs specific strategies and methods to realize our vision—our hopes and dreams to achieve our goals. This is why you need to prove your value.

I want to share with you the genesis of this mindset—the immigrant story of America. Think of it not as a history lesson but as an inspirational lesson. I came to America to make my own mark in life, but I didn't actually know much about the immigrant history in this country until I arrived here.

Except for my sister, my family and friends were on the other side of the world, and I was in this foreign country, in an entirely different culture—different language, customs, foods, and religions—it was definitely overwhelming at times. That's when I realized I was part of something that transcended myself, and it made me less nervous and less lonely. I was part of a long and continuous line of brave, ambitious people who made their way in this life on their own terms. That's what I wanted for myself, and that's what I want for you—even if you're not first-generation yourself.

Up until now, I've been talking about the First Generation Mindset as if it's specific to a particular group of people, that you somehow have to come to America as a first-generation immigrant to have this mindset. But this isn't the case at all, far from it. Anybody can have a First Generation Mindset. By having a vision, creating value, and making the "ask," you, too, can use this mindset for your success. And as much as I can claim first-generation status, I didn't really acquire a First Generation Mindset until I had been here for a number of years and put a name to what I realized helped me persevere through the hardships of building a new and successful life.

When I was interviewing for a job in college, Deloitte was the most sought-after company for people seeking to work in that field. For me to get that job, that was my "ask." My vision was to get employment in America and elevate my value, so I needed to work for a valuable company. When I interviewed for the job amongst more than 300 students, I was the only one with a 3.8 GPA. I was the only one who was a Certified Internal Auditor (CIA). And I was the only Certified Information Systems Auditor (CISA). With that profile, my value to the company increased, and my "ask" to get that job became easier.

That's how I ended up in Houston, working for Deloitte. I then transitioned into working in the oil & gas industry, where I would travel offshore to oil rigs and do operational and safety audits. It was a tiring job because I'd go for long stretches out to these rigs and work every day for weeks on end. When I returned home to Houston, I'd get a number of weeks off, often up to a month. With such an odd schedule, it was tough to settle into a groove—the time working was too long, but then the time off was too long as well. I again had a vision to change my life, so I decided to take up real estate to earn extra money during my downtime. I had a vision to be financially independent. I had a vision of being in control.

I earned my real estate license and began selling real estate as a part-time Realtor when I wasn't off on trips to the oil rigs. In my first year, I earned ~$63,000 as a part-time realtor. And at that time, my base salary at the oil and gas company was about $93,000 a year. My wife and I were trying to settle down and start a family, and so I told my manager that I was seeking a pay raise that would bring me to $100,000 the following year.

When I received my pay raise, my base salary did go up—to $99,987. Something in me snapped. It was only $13.00 short of what I had asked for, but that $13.00 felt like a slap on the face, like I was being sent a message that someone else was ultimately in control of how much I made and when I made it. In hindsight, I realize this was an overreaction, but, at the time, it brought out in me all the passion and determination that I originally had when I came to America. I remembered that I didn't want to work for someone else. I didn't want to have my entire life scheduled around a corporate timetable that had nothing to do with who I was or what I wanted in life. My manager shorting me that measly $13.00 screamed this all out to me at that moment.

I made up my mind right then and there that I would quit being an employee.. Earning that ~$63,000 doing real estate the year prior gave me the confidence to think I could do this all on my own. But there was one big factor left to consider: I needed the blessing of my wife, who is both my partner and my support system in all of this. She generously gave me her blessing and support, as she always has. Based on my ethnic background, we are risk averse. Being a doctor, being an engineer is the right path to success, according to my culture. So, my deviating from those "accepted" career paths was a huge, huge decision.

When I spoke to my parents, they said, "Are you sure? You came to America, went to graduate school, and earned your Master's Degree. Do you really want to be a Realtor?" Because back in India, most people are risk averse. My family is risk averse. On top of that, the profession of real estate agents in India is not admired; it's looked down upon. In fact, Realtors are actually called "Property Dealers" in India; for lack of a better word, they're considered borderline crooks.

But I was committed. And I believed in myself, in my skills, and in what I could do. And so importantly, I had the support of my wife. And that was it. I quit my job and went all-in on real estate to start my own business and chart my own path. It was again a small story—a $13.00 story, to be exact—but harnessing my First Generation Mindset at that time changed the entire course of my life. My hope is that reading this book will change yours as well.

CHAPTER 2

How to Use the First-Generation Mindset for the Future

Clarity of Vision

Most people are driven based on the goals they outline for themselves. A goal to have financial success, a certain size of home, living in a certain neighborhood, or driving a certain kind of car. Goals have a finite deadline and a finite finish line, which, once accomplished, makes more people depressed than happy because, most of the time, these people lose a sense of purpose. That's why we say when a lot of people retire or stop working, they lose their purpose in life, and they get depressed.

On the other hand, vision is so big, so far out, that you never, ever reach the finish line. Vision is the ability to think about a plan for the future with imagination or wisdom. And that's why having clarity of vision is key to being successful. Without clarity of vision, you may have success, but it's going to be limited. Success will be driven by your environment, the people you work with, your friends, and family members. But when you're vision-driven, you always think about the future and what you can accomplish, with or without resources.

So for me, my vision is to leave a legacy of impact. Legacy of impact means that when I'm gone—ten years, twenty years, or fifty years from today—I'll be remembered as somebody who impacted not just the local market, the Texas market, but the US market. I want to be remembered as someone who came as an immigrant to this country with a whole lot of nothing, and was able to help the real estate industry and help entrepreneurs succeed. My vision deadline or finish line is so far out that I will never, ever reach the finish line. And that's what true vision is all about. It needs to be so big and so far out that you keep working hard on a daily basis to accomplish your vision.

Now to meet your vision, it has to be where you're visualizing yourself, accomplishing something that most people think is not going to happen. When I was a brand new agent, I went to a conference in Dallas, and I was receiving an award based on production, or commission, that I had earned the previous year. According to those production level awards, I was receiving the lowest level award. And I didn't get to go on stage for that award, but at the same event, the same real estate conference, an agent got to go on stage to receive the award for the Rising Star in the State of Texas. And when she walked across the stage, I said, "Wow, I'm going to walk the stage next year with the same award as the Rising Star Award, State of Texas."

I visualized myself walking across that stage. At that moment, I did not know what it would take or what I had to do to accomplish that vision, but it didn't matter. I would visualize it first and figure it out later.

I came back to Houston, went to the owner of my real estate brokerage, and said, "Tell me about this Rising Star award!"

He told me, "Kunal, for that, you've got to earn at least $250,000, plus you have to do all these things," and proceeded to name off several other actions I would need to take. Did I mention it was also my first year in 2014 as a full-time Realtor? And I said to him, "You know what? I'm going to win Rising Star Award this year."

He looked at me and smirked at me, and made me feel as though I was being a dumb fool for even setting that goal to win the Rising Star Award. And that face, that smirk, I haven't ever forgotten it. It's been almost 10 years, and I still remember.

I left his office, went back to my office, and told my business partner—my brother-in-law Sonit—that I would win the Rising Star Award. To make that a reality, I needed to earn $250,000 along with the other things mentioned by my broker. However, based on our business agreement, if I was to earn a quarter million, Sonit would also need to earn a quarter million. That meant to win we had to earn over $500,000 as a team. Now, as a brand new real estate team, earning $500,000 in the Real Estate business had yet to be done because it's extremely challenging. But that year, with our team's effort, we closed about $28 million in sales volume. We earned about $575,000 in commission, and I won that Rising Star Award.

It started off with me visualizing myself walking across that stage. I thought that if that other person had done it and got the award, there was no reason I couldn't win it next year. The roadblocks thrown at me by my broker were like a challenge for me. Tell me I can't do it, and I'll prove you wrong. Winning the Rising Star award was not necessarily a way to prove him wrong, but to prove to myself that while being new in the business, I could do whatever it takes. And that was one small milestone that I accomplished in 2014.

Since that year of being successful as a Realtor, as the Rising Star, I have not looked back. I set my own milestone goals or milestone accomplishments every year, and once I reach them, then I set higher goals. But overall, I'm driven by my larger, end-of-life vision. I'm not driven by my financial goals one year over the next year. Why? Because what happens is when somebody, especially within sales, sets up their goal for the month, for the quarter, or for the year to make so many sales or earn so much money, they get into complacency mode once they reach those goals. They forget about the big picture of why they first got into the business.

For me, coming to America was a huge privilege. In India, we have over 1.4 billion people. Coming to America is a golden ticket, an opportunity that very few are given. For the ones who are able to, a lot of them get into the nine-to-five grind to make ends meet or live a life of complacency or live a life that's low risk. After I came to America, I spent a good share of time—over a decade—working in corporate America, nine to five, but I had the desire to do more. I had the vision to be in control of my future, never to allow anything or anyone to stand between me or my financial goals. That's why I had to have such a big vision to really make it.

Over the years, my vision has changed. It has evolved. During my first year as a Realtor, my vision was to walk across the stage and receive that award. Once I accomplished that, the next vision was to be a preferred partner with builders. But overall, my vision was and still is to have financial independence and an amount that I can generate daily that far exceeds my financial expenses.

Now, the question is, how do you visualize your success in a way that will help you accomplish what you truly want? How do you visualize your future? How do you visualize your passion, and how do you go about accomplishing them on a day-to-day basis? For me, it all comes down to the reason why you wake up every morning. What's the thing that drives you? If you made an extra dollar today, what does that do for you? Why is it important for you to have the extra money in the bank? Is it to have a financial safety net, financial security, to provide for your family, to provide for your friends, or to give a better life to your kids and family members? There always has to be a reason why you're doing certain things.

How to Deal with Mental Roadblocks

Most people have mental roadblocks. These mental roadblocks are, in other words, limiting beliefs you've mostly created yourself. You create your own mental blocks, all limiting beliefs, but these mental roadblocks are often instilled in you by external forces. Often by very well-meaning people like your family or close friends. Your family members make you think with limiting beliefs because we are, as humans, wired to play it safe. We are wired not to take risks. We are wired to remain in a position that allows us to feel we are caring for ourselves and our loved ones. And the ones who take risks put a lot at stake. So your friends or family members, who really are trying to just protect you by playing it safe, might question you. And you are told by family members, "Hey, why do you want to quit your job? Why do you want to take this risk? Why do you want to start this business?" They do this out of fear of you failing—and they don't want that to fall on you. But when you fall into the trap of listening to others impose their limiting beliefs on you, you're allowing them to control your life. So, if your vision is to have an impact on your market, these limiting beliefs that you put on yourself or are there from other people, they become the biggest roadblocks that stand between you and your financial independence.

When I left corporate America and got into real estate, I was told that most realtors have to "put in their time" to get noticed and find real success. And maybe then you would be on people's radar because the real estate business is considered a "metaphase business," which means that you have to put in your time to be recognized. That's where I disagreed with all of them. I didn't verbalize that, but I shot all of that down in my mind. I said to myself, "I don't care how long others have been a Realtor. I believe in being a service-based provider. If I provide good services to my clients, to the industry, to my builder partners, or to other Realtors, I'll be valued. And if I'm valued, then I'll have more success in the market."

The limiting belief that is instilled in the Realtor profession is that if you sell so many homes, and earn so much commission, then and only then can you be considered successful. So what I did instead when I started as a brand new agent in 2014 was case-studied and evaluated all the top Realtors in the Houston market. I noticed they all had one thing in common: they had preferred status with builders. That means that when a potential buyer walks into a sales office interested in building a new home, you would typically have a builder salesperson who talks about the community, the floor plans, and all the other relevant things. And then, if the buyer was not working with a Realtor and wanted to buy a home and sell their home, they would be referred to the builder's preferred Realtors.

When I case-studied all the top Realtors in my market, I found they had preferred status with builders and received a lot of referrals for business that way. I wanted a piece of that action too. That was my vision back then that I wanted to be a preferred Realtor with these top builders. Now, they're not just going to give me a preferred status because I walked in and asked for it. I had to demonstrate my value to them.

I had to figure out what the gap was between my vision and my value, in other words, where I wanted to be and what I was actually bringing to the table. That gap analysis made clear that I had to elevate my value in the market to these builders. I also had to improve upon what the other preferred Realtors were currently doing and figure out a way to provide these builders with something they weren't expecting. I clearly outlined certain things that my team or I could do to elevate our value so that, in the end, we would be well-positioned to make our "ask" to become preferred partners with these builders, with the value to back up what we were asking.

In 2014, we targeted the top-selling neighborhood in all of Houston (and number five or six in the whole country), Riverstone Community. Every day, rain or shine, Saturday or Sunday, Monday or Tuesday, I was either at my Real Estate office or walking through homes under construction in the neighborhood, learning about the product lines, doing everything I could to elevate my knowledge and elevate my value.

Within 12 months, at the end of 2014, The Seth Brothers Real Estate Team was recognized. We received the award for being the top-selling team in Riverstone. That was part of our strategy to elevate our value to the builders there. Having received the award, the builders started to notice us and approached us about being their preferred Realtor team. In this case, we did not even ask for it, but the value that we added to the market made us valuable in the market.

Some people rely on people's words and accept that things are just done in a certain way because that's the way they've always been done. Like the idea that you have to have so many years of experience in the field, or do this, do that, to even ask for what you want to be accomplished. I'm here to tell you that's simply not the case. You control how far you reach and whether or not you make it to where you want to be. Don't fall into the trap of going straight for the "ask," either. Instead, find the gap between where you are now and what value you could add to your market and find a way to elevate that value. Then your "ask" becomes so much easier.

The roadblocks that you have in your life, whether they are instilled in you by your family members, by your environment, or by other things around you, put them aside and instead be driven by a big vision because when you're vision-driven, the only person that stands between you your accomplishments is *you*.

CHAPTER 3

Putting Vision into Practice

Time, Effort, and Hardwork

In the preceding chapters, I've written about the importance of having a clear vision as part of a "First Generation Mindset" and shared some examples about my vision, how I came about them, the obstacles I overcame to keep them in sight, and how that ultimately paid off for me with the success I always dreamed of having when I came to this country.

Putting your vision into practice is perhaps the most challenging aspect of being successful. Here's a great example: Elon Musk, the founder of PayPal, among other things, is considered a great visionary. He dreams of making humans a multiplanetary species—which is clearly a massive undertaking. When he ultimately sold PayPal to eBay for $1.5 billion in 2002, do you think he stopped there? No, he did not. He went on to found a new company, Tesla, which was also a huge success and generated an incredible amount of income and revenue. Did he then stop there? No, he's now focused on his SpaceX company, which he plans to use to colonize Mars, bringing him closer to his overall vision, step by step.

The key point in that example is that someone like Elon Musk has such a big vision that even selling a giant company like PayPal for $1.5 billion did not put him in the backseat or in complacency mode. It compelled him farther along his path, launching him closer to seeing his vision realized. Whereas most people in this world may have taken that huge paycheck and decided it was "enough," Musk was even more motivated to continue and reach even higher the next time with Tesla and then SpaceX. His vision is so big that he will probably never "finish." Do you think Musk will stop once SpaceX makes it to Mars and colonizes it? No, he will find other planets to go to and move on to the next big thing. I mentioned previously that your vision should be so big that you never truly "get there," you just keep expanding it as you go and reach milestones along the way that propel you farther along. Musk understands this concept and is the embodiment of this idea.

When a vision drives you, the only person standing between you and your movement toward that vision is yourself. The limiting beliefs and the limiting factors, no matter what they are and where they come from, are the only true obstacles in your way. You must overcome all hurdles through sheer determination, hard work, and believing that you can do anything you truly put your mind to.

Elon Musk is a very hard-working person who has even been known to sleep on the floor in his Tesla factory.

Why does he do that? Because that's his vision. He will do whatever it takes, and he sets an example for others to follow by embodying the hard work that he expects.

My personal vision has evolved over the years, as all visions should. When I came to America, my vision was to get a job, get a work visa sponsorship, and then move from a student visa to a work visa and be able to earn a good living. But I realized after accomplishing all of those things that I *thought* were my ultimate goals, I still had more to accomplish.

I then wanted to be self-employed, to be an entrepreneur, to be in control of myself. My previous professional accomplishments were just small steps toward this larger vision, which needed to be achieved for me even to realize that I wanted more. After transitioning to becoming a successful Realtor, my vision changed again. My purpose now, my even larger vision, is to impact more entrepreneurs, make them more successful, and allow others to envision something bigger and better for themselves.

In the last several years of being in the real estate industry, I've impacted hundreds of Realtors to help them be more successful. Having done that, my larger vision still needs to be accomplished and continues to expand. Now, my vision is to impact and influence entrepreneurs, not just Realtors, on a global level. To accomplish that vision, I'm in the process, at the time of writing this book, of building a commercial project in Houston, a three-story building with about 21,000 square feet.

On the first floor, we will have an event space, the second floor is a co-working space for business owners and entrepreneurs who need an office area, and the third floor is designed as a conference and training center. The vision and idea behind this building are to make it a center for sharing knowledge, expertise, and building on one another's strengths. To make us all more successful through our collective hard-working spirits and drive toward accomplishing our visions.

The name of the building is SETH, which stands for *Successful Entrepreneurs Transformed Here*. The plan for this location is to bring speakers, industry leaders, and experts to train other people to be more successful entrepreneurs and share their knowledge and wisdom. The main purpose is to help people in a nine-to-five job who may have a passion or vision to be self-employed or entrepreneurs to take that leap that gets them to the next step of their vision. To help them hear from others who have been in their shoes and overcame the limiting mindset that is far too easy to listen to, to realize that they too can keep pushing toward their visions.

Does my vision of building a center for entrepreneurs sound lofty? Of course it does, and that's exactly the point. Does my vision stop there? If you've read this far, you'll know that this is only the first step of many. Remember, your vision should constantly expand so you always reach for the next, better thing that makes you more and more successful. In fact, once the SETH building is complete, I will find another location to build another SETH, another SETH after that, and another SETH after that one. Do you think I will stop building this strategy after I've saturated the Houston market or even the Texas market? No, I will keep going and expanding, and that's what vision is all about. When you have a vision that helps people be the best they can be and reach their success, you keep going and keep expanding, no matter what. That's the point of vision.

Think about some of the top Olympic-level athletes of our time, Michael Phelps and Usain Bolt. To get to where they are and to be the best at what they do, they put in the hard work and have the discipline to keep going and keep pushing to do better. Whether or not they had a winning or record-setting time in their events, both Phelps and Bolt committed to settling for nothing less than greatness and focused on getting there through the things they *could* control: hard work and discipline—never giving up. They had the vision of being the best.

Your finish line, when you're vision-driven, is infinite, whereas most goals are finite (which was discussed in Chapter 2). Let's take baseball as an example. There are nine innings (though yes, you can go into extra innings). There are so many pitchers, so many people who come to bat. And then, eventually, that game comes to an end. There is going to be one winner and one loser. Winning the game would be an example of a goal.

Compare this to vision, where it's not about you winning or you losing a particular game or even getting a head start against somebody else. Vision is about staying true to yourself and what you *really* want on a daily basis, regularly, and doing whatever it takes to accomplish that, not letting any of the inevitable roadblocks along the way deter you from that. Being vision-driven means you don't just want to win the game, but you want to be inducted into the Hall of Fame and influence other players someday.

In my case, when building my THE SETH project in Houston, I faced roadblocks from day one, which I expected. Due to fire and building codes, designing a multipurpose space with offices on one floor and a training center on another resulted in unique challenges. Being required to have a certain number of dedicated parking spaces, certain safety features, and exits, making sure I complied with all building codes took some extra time and planning—and some headaches, too!

Now, some of these issues were easy enough to find solutions for. Extra staircases and wider hallways to accommodate larger crowds of people for conferences are easy enough to do, though at a cost ($100,000 in my case!). Other things, such as the parking situation, required more creativity and coming up with out-of-the-box solutions. Having vision means sometimes having to do things unconventionally, and being able to see around the roadblocks that seek to deter you away from your vision or even feeling like you need to scale it down.

The parking situation at the actual SETH building couldn't be changed. I had a certain allotment of space that could be divided into several parking spots without room for more. However, other offices and businesses along the same street also had their parking spots. I spent time going to each and every one of them, discussing my vision and what I was trying to accomplish with the SETH building. I knew that most of the conferences held there would be outside of normal business operating hours, so the businesses I was approaching wouldn't require the use of their own parking spots during those times. And I didn't stop there. Nothing will stand between me and my vision, my First Generation Mindset.

I continued looking for creative solutions to gain more parking available for the conference center. Across the street from the SETH building is the University of Houston. I contacted the business school there and devised a partnership with them that would benefit everyone in creating an entrepreneurial program. The business school will send students to our building, and they will have the opportunity to be trained, coached, and mentored by successful entrepreneurs. I faced a roadblock in needing more parking availability. Through determination and not giving up, I found a way to add value to someone (the university) to make my ask. And it paid off, not just for me but also for the business students.

There will always be roadblocks along the way of any path you choose to pursue, and realizing that they are not immovable is key to pursuing your big vision. As you've seen with all of my examples so far, when I've been faced with a hurdle, I've done the work and research to be able to add value to the person that can remove that hurdle to make it easier to make my ask (and I know that the answer is likely a yes!). You should be driven enough by your vision that you always find a way to keep going and never give up when things become difficult, or the unexpected gets in your way.

As I mentioned earlier, my big vision is to make entrepreneurs more successful and to give them clarity in their own visions. My vision is to help people transition from their steady nine-to-five jobs and take the risk to be in control of their future and to see that it can be done and it is possible. By providing the environment to facilitate this, I'm not only making progress toward my vision but helping others progress toward theirs as well.

We all learned during the COVID-19 pandemic that many things can be done virtually, be it with Zoom or other conferencing platforms, but in-person interaction, face-to-face meetings, and the energy that you feel from being around other people is second to none. Attending an in-person sporting event is a markedly different (and more exciting!) experience than simply watching it on TV in your home. It's the same when it comes to being around other business-minded people and entrepreneurs who are all there striving to be the best they can be, helping and encouraging others to do the same.

Putting my hard-earned equity into the SETH project, investing (if you will) in other people by creating a specific and encouraging environment, will have a great impact on others reaching success in their lives. I may impact one person or 10,000 people in a matter of a year or five years, or even ten years, but what really matters is that I'm working toward my vision and what I want out of my life.

Going back to my Elon Musk example, with his vision to colonize Mars and then other planets following that, SpaceX and Tesla are just tools to get there. That's what the SETH space is for me. A tool to move closer to my ultimate vision of helping and encouraging others to have the courage to follow their true passions in life. I'm not driven by how much money I earn as a successful real estate agent. Yes, I do very well financially, and I make money that allows me to acquire more assets. But that is not vision-driven. That is goal-driven. If I can impact entrepreneurs to be more successful, I'm working toward leaving a legacy and accomplishing my vision.

Another example of a rather unconventional way I'm progressing toward my vision of helping others achieve and be more: honoring the hard-working contractors, electricians, plumbers, roofers, landscapers, and others, who are physically making the SETH building a reality. There will be a wall on the exterior of the building where the name of every person who worked on my building will appear. Because of their help, hard work, and skills I will accomplish my vision of leaving a mark and having something of value, something that I can pass on to my kids and grandkids. I want them to leave their mark as well. How many buildings or projects have these people been involved with without ever really receiving credit for their work? Probably too many to count. I wanted to allow them to leave their own legacies behind and have something to show for their work. Ten years from today, they can always come to the SETH building, look at their name, show it to their kids and their grandkids, and say, "You know what, Daddy (or Mommy) built this building."

Here's the difference between accomplishing a goal or working toward a vision: building an asset (or an actual building, in my case) is a goal, but leaving an impact (by having and using the building) is a vision. A goal is finite, achievable, and then it's over. A vision has no finish line and no deadline. With a vision, once you get to the next step, you keep going and thinking bigger and bigger for the next step. So if you want to be truly successful, you must have a vision in place, and you must put that vision to practice and keep going at all costs.

I may not know how many more years I have left on this earth, but I know for a fact that every day I'm going to do *something* to be more successful. I will do something to work toward my vision of helping other entrepreneurs be more successful, showing people what it means to truly have a First Generation Mindset and never give up or become complacent. I'm playing the infinite game. If I can help someone and make them successful as an entrepreneur, their success will be passed on to their kids and grandkids. Now, they may never know who I was or what I did to make their grandfather or father or grandmother more successful as an entrepreneur, but I would feel blessed just to know that someone's life is better because of what I taught them, the wisdom I passed on to them.

As you work towards your own vision, there will be roadblocks—that's something you can count on. But what is important is to never lose sight of the fact that all roadblocks are temporary and can be overcome. Nothing is impossible.

Here's a final example of rising to the challenge of an obstacle when it stands between you and your vision: the story of how my valued Operations Manager revealed a roadblock I didn't even realize I had. My Operations Manager is one of my many employees who is a parent, and in this case, recently had twins. Being able to come and perform at work to help me build my vision requires parents to have consistent and quality childcare during working hours. They had recently had twin boys and were set to return to work when the childcare they had lined up fell through.

I desperately needed her back at work, but she wouldn't be able to return without someone to care for her children.

Being the vision-minded person I am, I began thinking of solutions to solve this issue. It got me thinking about how many of my other employees faced similar hardships with the issue of childcare. Having a three-story building "in my pocket" allowed me to devise a creative solution: opening a daycare in the SETH building for my employees.

Well, that was a great solution, but with a childcare center comes a lot of other issues with roadblocks to be addressed. The first is specific and strict guidelines, policies, and procedures that must be followed. There are safety codes, fire codes, parking issues, staffing issues, insurance policies, and many issues to work out. At the time of writing this book, I'm sorting through these issues and working with the city to make this vision a reality so that I can continue to work toward my greater, overall vision as well. Not only would a childcare center be valuable to my employees, but those wishing to attend conferences at the SETH center to improve their lives could also utilize the childcare if needed. I know this daycare will become a reality because no obstacle is insurmountable, and nothing will stop me from accomplishing what I set out to do. That's the First Generation Mindset.

The main point I want you to take from this chapter, from all the examples I've shared, is this: keep going. No matter what the obstacle, I keep moving forward and putting all of my efforts in one direction, the direction that gets me to my vision of helping others to find their own success. Many obstacles have appeared in my path since the day I arrived in this country as an immigrant looking for a better life, and I will tackle all of them, one at a time. If that means I'm spending money, time, effort, or resources, I will do that. That's what it ultimately means to put a vision into practice. Never stop reaching, striving, working for more, and most importantly, never give up, no matter what.

PART 2

VALUE

CHAPTER 4

Understanding Value

How to Evaluate Value

Value is a key component that bridges the gap between where you are today and where you want to be in the future. Without clarity on your value, advancing your life in a meaningful way, whether it be your career or some other measure, will be challenging. To further add value to yourself, it's important never to stop learning or seeking out new information—read books, learn, and elevate your knowledge base to keep bettering yourself.

My philosophy is you should be doing a gap analysis of what the market needs are, meaning what somebody else needs in terms of value that you could provide on an ongoing basis. Once you know the gaps, you must work hard to elevate your value to align with the other person's needs. So it becomes about adding value to the market, adding value to somebody else. And once you elevate your value and demonstrate that you possess the value that could fill someone else's "gap," you become *valuable*, and people will want to do business with you.

So when evaluating your value position, remember that the value you want to bring isn't necessarily what's important to *you*, but what the other party's needs are. For example, if you're working in my industry, real estate, with builders or developers, the value they seek is for Realtors to bring serious buyers to their sales office. Realtors are a liaison in transactions to make sure when a client buys a home that the transaction goes smoothly.

Now, if you want to ask for a sale from these builders, you must add value to them. Unless you identify the gaps—what needs to be done that is not currently done by others—there's no way you can elevate yourself to add value to them. You must identify the gaps.

So, how do you go about doing this? The first step is thinking from the other person's perspective: what would they value in their business? Once you evaluate what that value is to them, the next step is figuring out what you need to do to increase *your* value to align with what is expected. And then, finally, in the end, comes "the ask."

As I mentioned earlier, I did this with builders when I was a new Realtor. I made myself more valuable than other Realtors in the eyes of developers. I set about studying all of the top Realtors to see what could be done more effectively and efficiently and what the builders could use assistance with that they weren't getting from other Realtors at that time. I figured out through my gap analysis that these top Realtors were just showing up for the contract signing and then closing. That's it. They didn't assist the buyer along the way through the entire process, from pre-construction meetings, design center appointments, or anything else that came up along the way to give the buyers a top-notch customer service experience. They showed up for the bare minimum required to receive their paycheck and nothing more.

Once I discovered this and knew that I could provide a much better experience for buyers and bridge that gap between what others were currently doing and what I knew I could do better, I was confident that when I showed my value to the builders that we would have a much better "ask" to present to them. Showing them the value I could bring them made it much more likely that they would seriously consider making me a preferred Realtor partner.

The extra work I put in ultimately paid off, as I expected it would. Once we demonstrated our value to the builders we sought out, they made us their preferred Realtor partners. All I had to do was identify a gap I could fill for them and show them how I would do that (and then the other key part is making sure you actually *deliver* on the value you promise!). Being a preferred Realtor partner is a huge deal because it means we get referrals from our builder partners regularly without seeking out new business for ourselves. Every year since becoming a preferred builder partner, The Seth Brothers Real Estate Team has earned hundreds of thousands of dollars from these partnerships. All because I took the time and effort to find a way to add value to them.

Short Term vs. Long Term Thinking

Now, when you are figuring out the value you might bring to someone, it has to be long-term value, not just something that will be of benefit in the short term. What I mean by that is that just adding value by bringing buyers to a sales office is short-term because once the home is bought and the closing is complete, what's next? We found a way to further add value to our builder partners by developing product lines, training their sales team to work with new markets (like international buyers), developing pricing strategies, and more. We continue to change what we bring to the table and add more value each day to remain the best of the best—someone our builder partners *want* to stay partnered with for the long term.

There was certainly an immediate need in the Houston market for quality and committed Realtors to help the potential buyers coming to tour new construction homes. Still, we wanted to make sure that our value stretched beyond that immediate need and into the longer term.

This concept, thinking of adding longer-term value to our builder partners, wasn't something that other Realtors (even the successful ones who already had a preferred relationship with those builders) had done yet. I had a vision of adding tremendous value to our builder partners, so I researched what gaps I could continue to fill for them, even if they were blind to it. My team ultimately met with some national and statewide builders who had some challenges in the specific Houston market in which they were looking to build new homes. We brainstormed with them and shared information, various product lines, and floor plans that other builders in the area were using successfully.

They took that information and formulated a brand new offering that was more relevant to the market conditions and what the buyers in that area were expecting. As a result of those meetings and collaboration, the builders made millions of dollars in profits, thanks to our input. We certainly added the value we promised to them! What it didn't do was put any actual money into our pockets. We were not directly paid for the value we added; we were not paid for the time we spent. But the bond, the relationship that was built based on that partnership, has earned us partnerships at a national level. Our reputation as forward-thinkers and problem-solvers will continue to serve us and show our value for many years to come.

To reiterate, when you are looking to add value to someone—be it a builder, business, client, or anyone else—there are sometimes short-term needs, or gaps, that certainly need to be filled. But the more you think about the long-term value you can add to a prospective partner, the more true value you actually add. Steve Jobs, the founder of Apple Inc., is another great example of bridging the gap between where you currently are and where you want to be (your vision!) by increasing your value. Jobs had a vision of revolutionizing the cell phone industry. And when he first came out with the iPhone, the price was around $500. That price point was significantly more expensive than other cell phones in the market. At the same time, before launching the iPhone, Apple had already created the iPod, which was worth $200. With the release of the iPhone at a significantly higher price point, Job's strategy when speaking wasn't to say the price of it because the cost would've been an objection for most people when the other cell phones at that time were available for a lower price.

This was his marketing strategy: your iPhone will also allow you to store music, so you're replacing your iPod with the iPhone, which is a $200 value. Other cell phone brands in the market at that time were about $250-$300. So Job's offer with the iPhone was something to the effect of, "Well, the second value you're getting through this iPhone is a special feature which is the basic functionality of a phone. So that's another $300. If you have an iPod for music plus a cell phone, you're at $500 already. We're asking for $500 for a combined device with the convenience of not having to carry two separate things in your pocket. Even better, we've also made the iPhone with the capability of surfing the internet. Essentially a computer in your pocket. That's a 3-in-1 device and an excellent value for the price you're paying for an iPhone."

Essentially, he "value-stacked" his offerings with the iPhone. There was a feature to store music, a feature to make phone calls as a regular phone, and a third to surf the web. Based on the value stack advertised, despite the higher price tag, customers lined up outside of Apple stores to buy those iPhones because the value was made very clear to them.

So when you're strategizing creating a partnership with a prospective customer, figure out what would be of great value to them, assess the value gap (what they don't currently have that they would want), and then elevate the value of what you can offer them. That's when you'll find success in your endeavors.

Value and The First Generation Mindset

This strategy of understanding and elevating your value is a core principle behind the First Generation Mindset. When you first come to America, no matter what part of the world you come from—Asia, Africa, Europe—most people have a language barrier. Most countries don't have English as a first language. When you have a language barrier, you also have a cultural barrier. You don't always understand how the American culture works. You may not even be sure of how to dress for different situations in America. Those can be big barriers to success in this country as an immigrant. Those barriers create gaps between where people are and where they want to be. It's necessary to bridge those gaps by learning, finding the correct skills to offer people, and doing whatever it takes. Even in my case, when I first came to America 20 years ago, I initially came here to go to college, but I had my sights set on seeking employment to get sponsorship or a work permit. That was my "ask."

But if I had come to this country and asked for a job straight away, I would not have gotten employed. I had to figure out the gaps in my abilities and knowledge and what value I needed to demonstrate to truly be able to ask for employment anywhere. And those gaps in where I was and where I needed to be weren't difficult to figure out. First, I needed to complete higher education, graduate school, obtain the appropriate degree, have certain credits, a certain grade point average, and certain certifications. Then I knew I also had to be more effective with my English communication skills and learn how to dress appropriately for the type of work I envisioned obtaining.

So I had to bridge that gap between where I was and where I wanted to be, my vision. By the time I graduated from college, I had the right GPA, I had the right degree, I had the right certifications, and my value was elevated to what it needed to be. Then when I went to ask for the job I wanted, my "ask" became relatively simpler. The moral of this story: it's all about knowing where you need to add value and then doing it.

What this all means in terms of the First Generation Mindset, whether you're actually a first-generation

American, or a second, third, fourth, or fifth, is that somebody in your family came to America with a huge gap in the "value" they brought with them at the time of their immigration. They then worked tirelessly to bridge that gap-from language skills, from their (lack of) higher education or even the cultural gap. And then, as you move down generations, the hard work that went into bridging those gaps to adding value becomes easy for us to take for granted. We adopt a complacency mindset and stop reaching for more, stop striving toward and expanding our visions.

If you really want to progress and you want to get to the next level of success, you have to, on an ongoing basis, evaluate gaps, figure out how you can elevate your value to be relevant to somebody else, how you can add value to the market, to your customers, to the industry, and once you do that, success comes unfolding for you. That's the First Generation Mindset at work.

CHAPTER 5

How to Sell Your Value and Capitalize on It

Putting It All Together

Now that you have learned how to understand and increase your value in the previous two chapters, the question is, how do you "sell" your value to capitalize on what you bring to the table? The answer is probably not what you think because the answer to that question is that you don't actually *need* to sell your value. Instead, seek to sell your *vision*.

When you sell your vision, you're showing someone your perspective, allowing them to understand your vision better and align themselves with what you envision. When someone is aligned and on board with your vision, your value becomes worth even more to them in the partnership you are creating (your "ask" comes later after these other pieces are put together).

As I've mentioned several times, I have a big vision to help other like-minded entrepreneurs become more financially successful. That's what drives me. That vision is relevant to each and every person in this world. I believe that everyone has an "inner-entrepreneur" just waiting to be realized. Either they capitalize on it and put it to work, or they put it on the back burner and let it simmer away. People who are full-time entrepreneurs and do not have a nine-to-five job in addition to their entrepreneurial pursuits are following their dreams to be their own employer. Many people who work a regular job as an employee to have a steady income also have passions and dreams, whether it be music, writing, singing, or anything. They may have the vision to be able to follow their passions full-time but need the financial stability of working another job to get by and pay their bills. I believe that these "passion-driven" people also have an inner-entrepreneur, but have tucked it away to follow a "more realistic" career path at the sacrifice of their vision.

Now, the only way to truly achieve financial freedom in life is to be an entrepreneur, and getting in the right frame of mind to do that comes directly from having that First Generation Mindset. Recall that having a First Generation Mindset means that you take nothing for granted and stop at nothing to get where you envision yourself in the future—financial goals or otherwise. The First Generation Mindset mentality is truly realized when someone takes that leap of faith to become an entrepreneur, taking their destiny into their own hands.

It's so important for this group of people who have a passion for something, who have their own visions to become an entrepreneur in a way that aligns with their true passions, to find a way to adopt a First Generation Mindset and make that a reality. Taking that leap and selling someone on your vision to form a partnership that later allows you to make that "ask," to make your vision a reality, is a huge obstacle that many people find difficult to overcome. With a First Generation Mindset, nothing is impossible or insurmountable, so approaching obstacles, even perceived obstacles, with that in mind is what will allow you to succeed.

When you work for a company, you are never in 100% control unless it's your own company. If you're Elon Musk, you're in charge and call the shots in whatever way aligns with your vision at Tesla. But everyone who works for Musk is still at the mercy of the market, at the mercy of layers of management to have the job, to have the pay raise, or even to have employment in the future.

When you sell your vision to others to help them feel excited about a future that you envision and get on board with you, that's where you find long-term success. People like Elon Musk and Steve Jobs are visionary people, and that's what has revolutionized the auto industry and the cell phone industry. They didn't sell their values; they sold their visions. And that's what you need to do, regardless of your vision. Find the people who are as excited about your vision as you are and bring them along with you on your journey of realizing it.

Not too long ago, I was on an Uber ride. I asked the person driving the car, "What do you do when you are not driving Uber?" And she said, "You know what? I love being with kids. I want to open my own daycare, so right now, I'm doing childcare from my home, but I want to grow that business." And I asked her a lot of questions, "Why kids? And why is this your vision?" She answered that she has children of her own and she truly loves helping kids be more successful in life.

Her vision was to help other working parents have a nurturing and enriching environment they could rely upon when they needed to be at their jobs, knowing their children were in excellent hands. Since her daycare business was not making enough money to support her needs, she took on Uber driving to provide the income she needed to continue working towards her vision. After speaking with her and learning more about her vision and situation, I was confident that what she really needed was to take that final leap of faith, to ditch those "backup" plans that were actually detracting from her building her vision.

I talked to her about the First Generation Mindset, my vision, and how to truly sell her vision to others to pave the way for her own success toward her vision. That gave her a boost of confidence and validation in what she was doing and what she wanted to do. I hope that she took our conversation to heart and will find the will to overcome any obstacles in her path and make her dream daycare a reality. In the long run, I may never see her again, and I may never do business with her, but that quick Uber ride allowed me to give her some clarity on her path, fulfill *my* vision of helping others become successful entrepreneurs, and help us both work toward our visions at the same time.

I'm so clear about my vision that I could be talking to anyone, and I can relate to them and connect with them one way or the other by talking about their own vision. So when you craft your vision, craft it in such a way that it becomes your "elevator pitch"—your selling proposition to anyone in the market, whether locally in your city, state, or even globally. Your vision has to be powerful enough, big enough that it can impact humanity, impact people at a global level. So, when you are promoting yourself, don't sell your value; sell your vision.

When people first come to America, having that impact is what it's all about. They come with a vision to make a difference in their lives and the family members they left behind in their home country. And their vision is to elevate their value and then seek employment, get a job, make some money, and send the money back home. They're clear about their vision. Their vision is to be more financially successful, be financially independent, and not go back to their family members or their home country because they made it all the way to America.

That's what the First Generation Mindset is. When people come to America, they come with a vision of doing whatever it takes, and they must sell that vision daily, even if they don't realize that's what they're actually doing. Remember that you don't actually have to *be* a first-generation American to have the First Generation Mindset. The First Generation Mindset is something that will benefit everyone.

So, if you want to be successful, you first need to craft and believe in your vision message effectively, and then you've got to sell your vision on a daily basis. You will know very quickly which person, organization, client, and customer is aligned with your vision and will be on board with helping you achieve that. You want to work with people aligned with your vision, not with your value, or not with your "ask," because once you demonstrate value and meet their expectations, you become irrelevant to them. But when you are vision-driven, you always have something of value to add. So, capitalize on building your value and sell your vision effectively.

PART 3

ASK

CHAPTER 6

The History of the Ask — How People Approach the Ask

We All Have an Ask

As human beings, we all have wants, needs, and desires. We are always pursuing something that we do not currently have and are always trying to bridge that gap to get to our desired end goal. Most people do not succeed in their endeavors because their *vision* does not drive them. Instead, they're driven by their needs or wants. Conversely, when you have clarity of vision that you truly understand, and you work to increase your value before you make your "ask" for something that you want, the journey of getting to your destination of financial success, or getting that promotion, or starting a company, whatever your vision truly is, becomes much easier.

Let me explain with an example. As young adults, even as children, we are all taught and trained to be persistent. "Don't take no for an answer" and "Keep trying" are phrases that we hear over and over again. I personally completely disagree with that mindset. It's not about being persistent in getting what you want but rather about being clear about your vision—that is, ultimately, what's important and how you achieve success. When we're young, we need to go outside to play, so we ask our parents for permission to do so. We have a need, as young adults, to have a sleepover with friends or have a date night. Or we want to come home late one night after curfew or get a car. Those are all our wants and needs, and we are good at identifying and working towards those, even from a very young age.

But most of us never end up thinking past those basic things, beyond those wants and needs to what *vision* we have for our lives. That's why it's so important to stop and focus on your vision. A great example of that is in corporate America or really any typical work environment. Most employees generally seek one of four requests categorized under P2B2, a term I have coined: Promotion, Pay Raise, Bonus, Benefits. These are the most frequently requested.

A highly effective strategy when addressing one of these requests is to initiate the conversation by aligning of vision that the employee has in their partnership with the company and their position, the value they bring to the company in terms of the time and effort spent solving problems that benefit the company through their problem-solving efforts or innovations in their job. When presented in this manner, the request becomes significantly more persuasive and likely to receive a positive response.

It is essential to illustrate the value you have delivered thus far by highlighting your commitment, dependability, and strong work ethic. The critical aspect is ensuring that your perceived value to the employer and the company is congruent with their expectation of value.

When conveying your value, it is important to emphasize your past contributions such as, surpassing expectations, proactive planning, effective communication, and a commitment to sustain productivity. Additionally, your value proposition should encompass a comprehensive plan for continued delivery without compromising your future performance.

Let us delve deeper into the concealed essence, often overlooked by the majority of employees. The hidden treasure lies not only in comprehending the value anticipated by your employer but, more significantly in surpassing the confines of your job description and dedicating yourself consistently to the grander vision of your employer and the company as a whole. Mere adherence to your daily tasks and responsibilities falls short of what is required to truly distinguish yourself in the workforce. Instead, it is the art of consistently delivering unexpected value that will ensure that your 'asks' are not merely met but enthusiastically fulfilled. This subtle distinction is what helps make your 'ask' easily fulfilled.

Over the years, I've hired and recruited a lot of employees in my company, and there are always people that I see who are only there to clock in, clock out, over and over again. Every year, they come and ask for a pay raise. They ask for a promotion. Then, some other employees commit themselves to their jobs, align with the company's vision and exceed the expectations set forth in their job description.

Those committed employees are the ones who are excited every time I share my vision for the company's growth. And they share that vision with me. Then, when it's time for a promotion, a bonus, or a pay raise, those are the people who have a head start over the rest of the pack. They're made their value clear, and they understand their vision to share in the success of the company, and they work hard to be a part of it. So be clear about your vision and the value you bring to a partnership, to a relationship, to a transaction. Only then should you make an "ask."

Approach Matters

I'll share a story from my personal life to drive this point. About a month ago, I was at a conference in Tennessee, which had about 150 people. On the last day, we had a keynote speaker. He was a phenomenal, greatly inspirational speaker who has a track record of success. When he got off the stage, I approached him and said, "I want to spend about five minutes with you. Would you have some time?"

He said, "You know what? I can give you five minutes of my time when the session ends." So when the session ended, I said, "Okay, is this a good time for us to chat?" He said, "Sure, let's go." I proactively had my phone with me and the five-minute timer set. I told Brad as I put the phone in front of him, "If in 60 seconds or less I don't say things that are relevant to you or of value to you, we'll end the meeting. But if I say things relevant to you, we'll continue the meeting for up to five minutes. Worst case, you're going to lose five minutes. Best case, you lost a minute. Are you okay with that?" He looked at me as if to say, "Who the hell is this guy? I don't know what he will talk about, but hey, let's hear him out!"

So I timed myself, though I wasn't rushing through what I shared with him. I talked about not what my "ask" would be but what my vision was. I also shared with him what I thought his vision for growth was. At about 50 seconds, I paused and showed him my timer. I said, "Brad, have I piqued your interest enough? Should I continue? Or would you like to end the meeting?" He said, "No, no, no. Please continue." And then I spoke for another three and a half minutes. And within four minutes, I shared my vision in detail. During that time, I had demonstrated the value I have in my market, and then I objectively shared with him what my "ask" was in the partnership with Brad Lea.

He said, "This was great. You know what? Please take my cell phone number, and let's reconnect and talk in more detail." I did not go into that meeting to sell myself, sell my partnership, or "ask" what I wanted in that partnership. I instead focused on my value and what I would bring to the potential partnership. Then, I presented an "ask" once

I was well poised to show how it would mutually benefit both of our businesses.

Now, back in the day, before I had any clue about vision, value, and making an "ask," I may have gone directly to him and said, "Hey, Brad, here's what I want to do. What are your thoughts?" And he may very likely not have had any interest at all because that would have simply been me trying to get something from him. Most people are geared toward asking straight out what they want that meets their goals, what's good for them, and what they value. Instead, you need to show what value *you* can provide to the other person, why your visions are aligned, and why whatever it is you "ask" will benefit you both.

Even at that, when you do position yourself well to make your "ask," you then have to present yourself in such a way that you are bringing value to them within the question too. And that's exactly what I did with Brad. I said, "Here's this partnership, here's how it can bring success to you, and here's what's in it for me." And that meeting was powerful because, in five minutes or less,

I could demonstrate my vision and my value and then make my big "ask." That's a formula I follow all the time, whether I'm talking to my employees, my clients, customers, a new business partner, or I'm interviewing someone. That formula is the key to truly getting what you're asking for—*vision, value, then ask.*

When I interview someone for a job, I always ask them, "What's your vision? Where do you see yourself in five years, ten years? What's your background? Why did you get into this business? What did you do in school? What was your major? Why did you pick that major? Why'd you move to Houston? Why'd you live in this town? Why did you do this? Why, why, why, why, why, why?" And once I've asked all those "whys," I'm evaluating what their drivers are, and why they're sitting in front of me. Is it because they have a financial need and they just need any job to make ends meet, to pay their bills? Or are they truly driven and know about my and my company's vision? And then I share with them, "Okay, let me tell you about my vision." And by that time, I don't even talk about the position the person is interviewing for. I talk about my vision, and I try to get a sense of their alignment with my vision. Are they truly listening to what I'm saying? Are they truly seeing the value in my vision?

Then I'll ask, "Where do you see yourself aligned in my vision?" If I see alignment in vision and they have value, nine out of ten times, when I'm interviewing candidates, I will create positions/profiles within my company that are aligned with their strengths and their vision for growth. I don't hire people based on the job opening or the company's needs today. I hire people based on the alignment of vision and what value they bring. Using this model is a key reason why my business has been so successful and why I have some of the best and most dedicated employees out there. Our visions are aligned, and when "asks" come up, employees typically get the answers they want because of the vision and value aspects discussed above.

In fact, many times, I will see people apply for an administrative position in my company because they need the financial stability of that position, in contrast to a sales commission employee (Realtor). But they are often the ones who are actually wired to be in sales and would likely excel at that job. So over the years, I've created a hybrid position. I hire someone as a showing agent, where they get a base pay but a lower commission split because I'm taking on the expenses for various licensing and educational aspects required for those positions. Having that base pay to rely on while also adding a small commission allows them to move forward in their career and to transition eventually toward a full-time sales role. I make a path of success for them with evaluations along the way, and when the time is right for them, they can become full-time Realtors.

I've had people tear up and cry during these interviews where I explain this type of career pathway I offer employees because I help them pull out what their vision truly is. I pull out what value they have. They're there to ask for a job, but really they should be focused on vision and value first. When I go through that process with people, I often hear, "Nobody has ever talked to me like this, that they're more concerned about my value and my vision than what the needs of the company are. That's why

I would love to be part of this organization." And when I hire those people, they're "lifers" that join the company because we're aligned with our visions.

So no matter what position you are in, whether interviewing someone to join a company or interviewing to get a job, lead with a vision, talk about the value you bring to them, and then talk about the mutual growth and success you'll have with the partnership. Last of all comes that *"ask."* "Would you consider giving me a job? Would you consider giving me a pay raise? Would you consider giving me a few days off to spend with the family?" Switch your strategy to position yourself to have a stronger and better "ask," and you are much more likely to succeed. Craft your "ask" with a three-step process: vision, value, and finally, ask. You'll be surprised at how much more effective you will be when using this process!

CHAPTER 7

Believing in Your "Ask"

Now that we've discussed the "vision, value, ask" process and how implementing it is vital to the First Generation Mindset, there is an important caveat regarding the "ask"—you have to truly believe in what you're asking. And not just believe in what you're asking but understand that what you're asking for is aligned with the value you bring. To truly believe in your "ask," you should be honest with yourself about whether or not you genuinely deserve whatever it is you're asking of someone. That's a common mistake that people make. They believe in the "ask" itself more than they believe in the value they bring to the table. You can't just ask for something for the sake of getting it. The things you ask for should be a direct result of your vision and value. For example, if you work for an employer, you might ask for a promotion or pay raise. And when you do not get the pay raise or promotion, and somebody else gets promoted from your peer group, you should question why your "ask" was not fulfilled.

The main reason for the situation described above can be boiled down to two types of values: the value you *actually* bring to the table and the value you *think* you bring to the table. You may not be what your employers see your value as, and that mismatch can leave you in a tough spot. Similarly, the value that you bring to your employer may be different from the value your employer is actually seeking. The person who ultimately got that promotion you had your eye on may well have increased their value to the company in a way that you did not and also in a way that the employer valued over what you offered.

If you made the "ask" without having the proper value to back it up, it shouldn't be surprising that you did not receive the answer you expected. Instead, put in the time and effort to ensure that the value you bring to someone is as valuable to them as you think it is. Also, ensure that it's the specific value they're looking for. These steps will better position you to receive a favorable answer. By doing that, you can truly believe in your "ask" and it's not just an arbitrary thing you want.

I worked in corporate America for over a decade, and multiple times, I was passed up for promotions and pay raises. Understandably, I would get frustrated that my coworker got the promotion and I did not. Those experiences set me on the path to truly understanding why that was happening and what I could do about it. I eventually came to understand what the issue indeed was: the value *I* thought I was bringing to the company was not relevant or important to the employer. That's not to say that I wasn't valuable. What it means is that it wasn't the right kind of value for the situation. So when you are thinking about asking for a promotion, pay raise, or really anything else in life you want to make an "ask" for, you really need to go in believing in your "ask" and knowing you have the correct value behind it. If that value that you bring is not aligned with the employer or partner you are seeking out, go find another environment that *is* looking for what you offer. You can only value your "ask" when you believe in the value that you *know* you can provide to the person who *wants* it.

When people first come to America, they come here to seek employment, to find better lives for themselves and their families, looking for success that isn't possible in their home countries. They come here to seek the opportunity to earn citizenship, which takes years and years. Immigrants can find success and build those lives they seek by keeping that First Generation Mindset—working hard, never giving up, and following their vision by providing value and making true "asks" when they count. A deep belief in whatever it is they ask, be it employment, a new opportunity, or whatever, is what makes them successful in the end. Bringing value to the market in which they seek to enter, value to their employer, to their business partners, to know the "ask" is something worth asking. Adding new and improved skills, creating, getting more education, or learning new information are all ways to improve your value. But it's important to make sure the gains in value that you're making are the ones that are sought by whomever it is you're planning to make your "ask." You can only believe in your ask after believing in the value you bring to the table.

CHAPTER 8

Crafting and Applying "The Ask"

When you finally make it to the stage of presenting your "ask" to your client or prospect, by this point, the fulfillment of whatever it is you're asking for should come almost automatically from the person to whom you are presenting it. It shouldn't be the case that your "ask" gives someone pause or that it isn't immediately clear to them just how much value they could receive by helping you achieve your "ask." If you were not clear upfront about the value you were going to add to them, you need to go back to the drawing board and make sure you've properly set everything up for your "ask," all of which we've discussed in the previous chapters.

For anything that you do in your life, you always, always have an "ask." The methodology that I use of "vision, value, then ask" is ultimately all about getting your "ask" fulfilled, which is how you then get to the next step toward achieving your goals and realizing your big vision. You should do your due diligence and research ahead of time to be fully prepared to make an "ask" of anyone. Remember, you must clearly show someone how helping you will also help *them* like I did when I set out to become a preferred Realtor partner with certain builders (Chapter 4).

When you are truly ready to bring your "ask" in front of your intended audience, it should be so specific and well-crafted that the outcome should be, or will be, in your favor. You can't just go in and "wing" it or you will quickly find that you aren't getting the answer you want. But, if over a period of time, you have ensured that you bring value, you're capable of accomplishing what you say you will, you put in the effort and work—that you're someone worth partnering with—there's no reason why you should not get your "ask."

If you find that you're not successful in getting the results you want or expect after making your "ask," you need to take a step back and evaluate what's happening so you can regroup and try again once you have a better handle on what's going wrong. Typically, I've found that there are one or two reasons why your "ask" does not get fulfilled. Either 1) you were not crystal clear about your "ask" upfront with your prospect, or 2) you made assumptions that your prospect has inferred your value when instead you should have made sure that they were aware of and appreciated what you bring to the table (and therefore how they will also benefit).

You have to be vocal and clear about everything each step of the way. Never assume that anything is "understood" by the other party. Sometimes people take things for granted or don't realize that you are contributing to something as much as you are or have been. You should make sure you remind them of your value and what it means to them. Then when you're asking them to take another step in your professional relationship, you've already put in their minds that it would make a lot of sense to continue to be in a partnership with you. This might mean you say something to the effect of, "I believe when I first met with you, you had *this much* business share in the market. *These* were the missing pieces in your organization's network strategy. I believe I was able to add value to you by doing *one, two, three, four, five things*, and my "ask" for this partnership to grow further is that you consider doing business with me now in *x* because *y*."

Reiterating what your value has been over a period of time is the critical step. You want to clearly remind them of just how much they've already benefited from having you as a partner, which then makes it seem much more reasonable for them to consider continuing a partnership in other ways than you're now suggesting. Once you lay that out (and you've already demonstrated to them effectively what value you've added), there's no reason why your "ask" will not be fulfilled. It's all about effectively laying the groundwork first, then going in and asking for what you want. The set-up part is the crucial piece to getting the answer for which you're looking.

Your "ask" is the final step in the "vision, value, ask" process and its success really depends on how you've gone about setting up the first two steps: vision and value. You can't make a reasonable "ask" of someone if you can't also easily demonstrate the vision and value behind the "ask," so make sure to set yourself up properly to win when you've decided it's time to make an "ask" of someone. Had I just gone into a top builder's office and said, "I'd like to ask you to partner with me as a preferred Realtor," it's very unlikely I would have succeeded. However, when I went in, and was able to say, "I have the vision to create a hugely profitable partnership between my accomplished realty business and yourself, and I am extremely knowledgeable about your target market and products. My office has added x amount of revenue to builders such as yourself in the last year, and because of that, I'd like to form a partnership with you as your preferred Realtor," I made a much stronger case.

The main point and bottom line here: set yourself up for success. Do the work behind the scenes so you are confident that you are worth whatever it is you're going to ask for, and make that worth explicitly clear upfront. Don't leave it to chance that anyone recognizes your hard work, previous success, or value you bring to the table—be sure you remind them. Making a strong case for yourself before you make an "ask" means your chances of success are much higher!

CHAPTER 9

Honest Measurement and Accountability

Most people are driven by goals and vision, things they wish for or desire. Some people may want a certain amount of financial success, sell a certain amount of units of product each year, drive a certain type of car, or live in a certain kind of house. These are all things that one needs to work towards to make them a reality. But how do you know if you're going to reach your goals and ultimately attain your big vision?

Without a system in place to measure or keep yourself accountable for the steps needed to move you closer to your vision, it's unlikely you will ever realize it. It's important to know not only what your big overall vision is but what benchmarks and goals you need to meet to reach it, and that's the piece that many people often miss when they think about achieving something. If you want to have a certain amount of money in the bank, what small steps do you need to accomplish along the way, and in what timeframe? If you have your sights set on a certain kind of car, how would you make that a reality?

When you have a big vision for your life, you eventually accomplish it by having a set of goals aligned with that vision. The goals hold you accountable and measure the progress you make along the way. For example, suppose your vision is to have financial independence and success that far exceeds your lifestyle expenses on an ongoing basis. In that case, you will need to hit smaller benchmarks along the way. This might mean you set a goal of making "x" amount of money in the next year, and once you reach that, move the goal to "y" amount the following year. Having checkpoints in place allows you to constantly evaluate if you are on the right track or need to pivot and reassess your approach as you assess whether or not you are aligned with your vision. Assessing and evaluating is an essential and important part of meeting goals and reaching your eventual vision.

At a minimum, you need to be evaluating your progress on your goals on an annual basis. You need to set aside the time to sit down and look at each goal you've set for yourself and truthfully take a look at where you are in relation to that goal. If you're not where you want to be, delve into what happened (or didn't happen) and use that information to pivot or make changes to get back on the right track. While there's no definite timeline for reaching a big vision that you have in life, it is important to make sure that you are continually making progress towards it. The best way to do that is to set specific smaller goals along the way and consistently evaluate how you're doing to reach those goals annually. Knowing where you are on the journey of where you want to be makes it more likely that you will end up at your destination.

If your vision is to achieve financial success, how much do you want to have in your bank account at the end of this year to move the needle in that direction? How about the next year? Taking stock annually of where you are in relation to your vision will help you stay on the correct course. This is the case for any vision you have, not just financial or money-driven ones. Do you have a certain weight you'd like to be? Then how many pounds do you want to lose this year to work towards that? Keep yourself accountable to continue working toward your vision by checking in on your progress regularly with smaller, more easily achieved goals along the way.

Without checks in place, you will always be chasing your vision as an abstract idea that you wish for rather than an attainable endpoint that you can eventually reach. You'll always be chasing the extra dollar, chasing the success of driving a nicer car, living in a bigger home, or losing that weight you want to get off. So take a timeout. Solidly define the vision that you want for yourself. What's really interesting about doing this is that you may set certain goals for yourself that are aligned with that long-term vision accomplishment, but when you take an inventory, a lot of times you may have to tweak or broaden the horizon of your vision, which then ultimately leads to you needing to change or realign your goals. And that's perfectly acceptable and should happen as you gain more clarity on your vision and where you want to go in life. So on an ongoing basis, have an honest measurement system in place and hold yourself accountable to the goals that you've set that accomplish that bigger vision. Those smaller steps are what will ultimately allow you to end up taking the bigger leap.

CHAPTER 10

Updating Your Vision and Crafting Your Legacy

Take Inventory Every Five Years

When you think about having goals, perhaps one of the most important, though often overlooked, aspects is the fact that goals can be adjusted and realigned as you progress in your professional career and your life. In the same way, your big vision needs to be accounted for and updated regularly as well. When you do this, you're primarily building your vision in such a way that you can leave a legacy after you're gone—which is one of the most important reasons you're working hard towards a big vision in the first place.

There are quite a few powerful examples of very successful people who have done this themselves. They adapted and changed goals and visions as they progressed on their road to success. Goal-driven people who were also clear about their big vision, and through that vision, they have and will continue to leave a legacy in this world. For example, let's go back to Steve Jobs. He was a goal-driven person who was clear about his vision to change how we communicate and the role telecommunication would eventually play in our lives. Not to mention also being the visionary behind Apple Computer, iPhones, and iTunes—all products he envisioned to change the world—and reasons why he left such a powerful legacy.

Another great example is someone else I've mentioned, Elon Musk. With Tesla, he wanted to change the automobile industry, having a big vision behind the brand to revolutionize cars. After largely accomplishing that, Tesla is an internationally known and respected brand.

His next vision is to take humans to the planet Mars. Musk is envisioning the next big step for humans to take. It's doubtful that he had that in mind when creating Tesla, but as time went on, he continued to re-craft or update his vision. The legacy he will leave behind is someone who revolutionized transportation and how we explore the world—and beyond!

In the computer world, Bill Gates introduced Microsoft Office, Excel, and Word. They are all the tools that most computers have in place today and are household names when it comes to doing just about anything electronically. After becoming very financially successful, Gates shifted his focus to philanthropy and used his success to make the world a better place for others. He's done this largely through his Bill and Melinda Gates Foundation, impacting people in Africa and other countries who do not have the financial means of getting fresh or clean water. This is how one leaves a legacy: being impactful to others through their big vision, which adapts over time.

Mark Zuckerberg with Facebook, now called Meta, is another example. His vision has changed the world in terms of how we communicate, how we share things about one another, and how we stay in touch with people you may not have seen in over 20 years or more. Social media allows us to stay connected and keep updated on what others are doing daily in ways that were unimaginable before it. We can see photos and updates of what our families and our kids are doing and even keep in the loop with local events and news matters. Through all of this, the initial vision of Facebook, and adapting and changing it over the years, Zuckerberg will be leaving a massive legacy.

The first-generation mindset, our focus throughout this book, is all about leaving a legacy and being remembered for the work you've done long after you are gone. Everyone is going to leave a legacy; not leaving one is not an option. You are going to leave a legacy behind whether you like it or not. Your legacy will last for 24 hours, 24 days, or forever. Are you leaving a legacy of impact?

That can only be possible if you are clear about your vision, set goals to achieve that vision, and work hard to get there—never giving up no matter what obstacles come your way. You need to be clear about what you are and how you will add value in the market while also making sure that others see and appreciate your value. Finally, you need to always keep in the back of your mind what your "ask" is and be ready to make it when the time is right. The "Vision, Value, Ask" process discussed throughout this book will lead you to craft your legacy and leave your impact.

Build out your vision today so that you can leave a legacy of impact for your next generation and show the world what someone with a first-generation mindset can accomplish when they set out to do something truly great!

BONUS CHAPTER

Cultural Training

In 2014, when I was a brand new Realtor, my big vision was to add value to local builders. And to that end, I developed a training program called, *How to Decode and Win Indian Clients.* My intention was that by adding value to specific builders, they would then be more likely to make me and my real estate team, The Seth Brothers "preferred Realtors". Recall from earlier that "preferred" status means that if a buyer goes into a sales office ready to buy a new home and sell their current one, and they're not already working with a Realtor, the builder would then refer that prospective buyer to one of their preferred

Realtors. Being a preferred Realtor with a new home builder leads to exponential success for real estate agents.

Now, as a brand new Realtor just starting out, I could not just go up to a builder and ask them to make me a preferred partner. I had to somehow add value to them to make that happen. I already had the clarity of my vision and what I wanted from it, but I needed to take steps to make it actually happen. The first step of that was adding value to the builders.

So in 2014, I was out working as a Realtor with some new construction homes, and I happened to bump into Vice President of Sales of a National Builder. I met him in a parking lot and I had maybe a minute or two to engage with him. During our conversation, he said to me, "Hey Kunal, I understand your team has sold a lot of homes to buyers from India. What do you know about them?"

So very quickly, I was able to demonstrate to him my knowledge base and expertise about working with buyers from India and how I could help his team get more sales with that specific part of the market. That clearly had relevance to him, and within a minute or two, I was able to effectively demonstrate to him that I was a subject matter expert in regards to Indian clients.

Next, The Vice President of Sales said, "In about two weeks, I'm doing a training citywide for all my communities, for all my sales team. Would you be able to come and train my team on how to work with clients from India?" I said, "Absolutely, yes." And for the next two weeks, I spent a lot of time and effort in developing the training program, which is called *How to Decode and Win Indian Clients*. And when I did the training, it was fantastic. We got great feedback, had great interaction with the builder salespeople, and all of that helped me add and demonstrate value to the builders.

And in time, six months after that training, the builder did approve my team to be preferred Realtors with The Builder. Now, in the last ten years, I have traveled nationwide doing similar training. I've trained builders and Realtors—thousands of them. A few to name are: Taylor Morrison Homes, Meritage Homes, Newmark Homes,

Darling Homes, Lennar Homes, Pulte Homes, Highland Homes, Perry Homes, Toll Brothers, Shea Homes—the list is long. I have also branched out and spoken at real estate conferences, trained lending teams, Title companies, construction managers, design studio consultants —and really anyone who works with a buyer from start to end.

My mindset is that there is plenty to go around for everyone (and I have an abundance mindset). Even though I'm the subject matter expert and I know about Indian clients more than anyone else, I'm willing to share my knowledge base and expertise with other people. I do this because I believe that if I'm adding value to builders or Realtors, they would like me more and see the value I can bring to them. If they like me more they'll trust me more, and then they'll eventually do business with me.

So again, the same concept about "Vision, Value, Ask" has been so relevant to my life, career, and success. In this example, my "ask" was to get preferred status as a Realtor for these builders, but they were not just going to hand it to me as a new Realtor just starting out back in 2014.

So I had to add value to them- which I did. And over the years, this training program that I created has been wildly successful. I get requests all the time from different divisions, different cities, different states where their sales team is struggling to work with Indian clients. They call me in and I do the training for them, continuing to add value to myself and my business.

The key point is that it's all about "Vision, Value, ask." Add value to other people and then your "ask" will be fulfilled as a result.

Made in the USA
Columbia, SC
14 October 2024